Unfolded Letters To Self

Tales of a Heart That Loved in Silence

G. Krishna Chaitanya

BookLeaf Publishing

India | USA | UK

Made with ❤ on the BookLeaf Publishing Platform
www.bookleafpub.in
www.bookleafpub.com

Dedication

Dedication

To all the shayars at heart,

the doston who listen to poetry over chai,

the dilwale who wear their emotions like a dupatta in
the wind,

and the mast maula souls who find jugni in every verse.

This is for the midnight scribblers,

the diary ke raazdaar,

the ones who find poetry in Mumbai local rush and old
Bollywood songs.

May these poems sit with you like an old friend,

steaming like adrak wali chai,

telling you stories of love, dukh, and a little bit of masti.

With love and a little extra tadka,

Chaitanya

Preface

Preface

Poetry has a way of sneaking into our lives—sometimes in the quiet of the night, sometimes in the middle of a busy street, and sometimes over a cutting chai with an old friend. It isn't just words on paper; it's emotions woven into rhythm, a song only the heart understands. This book is a collection of such moments—of love and heartbreak, of laughter and nostalgia, of dreams and dukh, all wrapped in verses that carry the essence of everyday life. From the chaos of city streets to the warmth of childhood memories, from unspoken confessions to the magic of first rains, these poems capture the little things that make life beautifully desi. If you have ever stared at the moon and sighed, if an old Bollywood song has made you misty-eyed, if you've found poetry in a mother's scolding or a friend's teasing —this book is for you. May these words feel like home, like that last sip of chai, like a long-lost tune you hum without realizing.

So, open these pages, and let's go on a journey together —one verse at a time.

With love and a little extra mehsoos,

Chaitanya

Acknowledgements

Acknowledgements

This book is not just mine—it carries the warmth, laughter, and love of many hearts.

First and foremost, my heartfelt gratitude to my family, who never questioned my endless scribbling on the last pages of notebooks and always believed in the power of my words. Your love and patience have been the ink to my pen.

To my friends—the late-night chai partners, the poetry ke silent admirers, and the ones who listened to my verses even when they made no sense—thank you for your endless encouragement, your teasing, and your unshakable faith in my dreams.

To my mentors and teachers, who taught me that poetry isn't just about rhyme but about emotions that flow beyond words—your guidance has shaped my voice in ways I cannot express.

A special thank you to every street corner, every Bollywood song, every rain-soaked evening, and every chai tapri that inspired these verses. Life itself has been the greatest muse, and I am forever grateful for the stories it whispers.

And finally, to you—the reader. Thank you for picking up this book, for giving these words a home in your heart.

May these poems find you at just the right moment and
stay with you like a familiar melody.
With all my love and shukriya,

Chaitanya

1. From Snack-Less Pack to Love on Track

I saw you there, all cool and grand, My heart said,
"Stop!" My feet said,
"Stand!"
But you, my dear, were on the move, While I was stuck
in a one-sided groove.
The train whistled,
"Choo-choo, bye!"
I waved and shouted,
"Wait! Oh, why?" You smiled and left, no looking back,
Now I'm here with a snack-less pack.
They say, "Miss a train for love, it's fine,"
But my love story? A big fat whine!
I missed the train, I missed my chance, Now I'm stuck
doing a solo dance.
But wait! What's this? A twist in the tale,
You missed the train too,
• and turned quite pale.
You saw me there, all sad
and blue,

And realized your love for me was true!
Oh, love, you're like a delayed express,
Full of chaos, nothing
less.
But sometimes, missing the train's a win,
When it leads to love that's genuine.
Now we're here, hand in
hand,
Laughing at the train we didn't command.
You're the chai I finally
sipped,
The pakora that didn't
slip.
Desi style, short and sweet,
Love's a joke, but still a treat.
If you miss the train, don't despair, Another one's
coming-just be aware!

2. Chai, Toast, and a Love I Lost

I met you when wasn't keen,
Just sipping chai, all nice and clean, You came like a
masala twist,
Shook up my world, couldn't resist!
You danced in like o filmi scene,
With drama, laughter, full routine,
But your, l wasn't quite that smart, To handle matters of
the heart!
I lost you when I loved you most,
Like burning roti-gone, just toast!
Held on tighter than my mom's dupatta, Now I'm left
with just this katta.
Now I sit with chai and think,
Next time, I'll catch love's wink,
But I won't chase it like a train-
That runs too fast in the monsoon rain!

3. Her Glow in the Gray

On that day, the skies were gray,
The winds howled fierce, the world at bay.
But in her eyes, a quiet glow,
A warmth that made the cold winds slow.
When all seemed lost, and shadows grew,
Her presence whispered, "I'm here with you."
Through storms und doubt, through darkest night,
She brought the calm, she was the light.
The world may turn, may rage, may fight, But in her
arms, it all felt right.
On April's day, I knew it then,
She was my peace, my love, my friend.

4. A Universe in Her Eyes

In a realm where beauty reigns supreme,
There walks a girl, a mesmerizing dream.
Even if Devadas becomes Kalidas to sing,
His words would falter, unable to bring
Justice to her grace,her captivating allure,
A sight so enchanting, so wonderfully pure.

Her eyes, like stars in the velvet sky,
Hold secrets and stories, yet untold, so shy.
Her smile, a beacon, lighting up the night,
With every curve, a symphony of delight.

Her voice, a melody, like a gentle breeze,
Whispering secrets among the trees.
Even if poets penned their finest verse,
Her beauty transcends, a universe to traverse.

For in her presence, words dare not roam,
Bound by the spell of her ethereal home.

Even if Devadas becomes Kalidas to proclaim,
Her beauty leaves them speechless, lost in its flame.

6

5. A Remedy Called You

In this world of stumbles and scrapes so true,
"Do you have a Band-Aid?" I ask of you.
I fell for you, my coordination askew,
Or was it love's mischief that I misconstrue?

Beauty as time, an eternal view,
In this moment, let our connection accrue.
A watch I wield, a challenge I cast,
To see how long this enchantment will last.

A feline grace, if you were a cat,
Purr-fectly fitting in my lap, imagine that.
Is it hot in here or chemistry's decree?
In the warmth of our bond, we find unity.

Like a cricket match, your triumphs I'd cheer,
A spectator for you, drawing near.
Are you a magician or spice's embrace?
In your presence, life gains a flavorful grace.

Laughter, they say, heals the soul,
Meeting you, the cure that makes me whole.
In life's ailments, a remedy so rare,
With you, love's laughter fills the air.

6. The Forgotten Page in Life's Grand Play

Oh, joyous day, behold the grand parade,
As they find a substitute, my accolades fade.
In the realm of replacements, I'm now a ghost,
Once essential, now forgotten, a bitter boast.

They dance with delight, a new partner in tow,
My absence embraced, like a long-lost foe.
Behold the transformation, so swift and sly,
As I'm replaced with ease, a casual goodbye.

The echoes of laughter, once shared with glee,
Now resonate elsewhere, away from me.
A puppeteer of emotions, they've found a new stage,
In this melodrama, I'm but a forgotten page.

No need for remorse, for I've been replaced,
In this theater of life, my role erased.
They've found a stand-in, a shiny new delight,
As I fade to shadows, out of their sight.

7. Echoes Unanswered, Love Unspoken

In shadows cast by hopeful light,
A heart extends, arms open wide.
Love's offerings, a silent plea,
Yet echoes fade, unanswered, free.

In lover's gaze or family tie,
He paints emotions, vast and high.
But silence reigns, a heavy cloak,
His whispered love, the words unspoken.

A yearning soul, a lonely dance,
His love unmet, a fleeting chance.
To be embraced, to feel seen,
In the void, he wonders, in between.

Yet strength emerges, from within,
For love's resilience, a hopeful spin.
He learns to cherish selfless art,
Even when echoes stay apart.

8. With Every Hope, I Dream of Her

In dreams he paints her, fair and true,
A girl of grace in skies so blue.
Eyes that shimmer like stars at night,
A smile that brings warmth, pure and bright.

Hair that dances with the wind's embrace,
Her laughter a melody, full of grace.
Heart so kind, a caring soul,
Completes his world, makes him whole.

In her, he seeks a kindred spirit's fire,
A love that lifts him higher and higher.
With every hope and expectation in sight,
He dreams of her, his guiding light.

9. The Sweet Ache of Letting Go

In her presence, memories dance,
A lesson in love, a fateful chance.
To forget the girl who taught it all,
Is a challenge that upon me falls.

Her gaze, a map of moments sweet,
In every glance, our hearts did meet.
Yet now I strive to bid adieu,
To love that's old, to start anew.

But as she stands before my eyes,
The struggle to forget belies.
For in her presence, love's flame rekindles,
A battle within, my heart unwinds.

To part with what she taught, a test,
A bittersweet ache within my chest.
For though she's here, yet far away,
I'll learn to let go, come what may.

10. One in a Thousand

I liked a girl, not for her many parts,
But for the way she moves my heart.
She's not a thousand things in one,
But one thing in a thousand, a rare one.

She's not a puzzle to be solved,
Or a list of traits to be tallied and told.
She's simply herself, unique and true,
And that's what draws me to her like a glue.

Her smile is bright, her laugh infectious,
And the way she speaks, oh so gracious.
Her kindness and compassion shine so bright,
And her spirit is as pure as the light.

She's not perfect, but that's okay,
For her imperfections make her sway.
They add to her beauty, they make her real,
And that's what makes her so surreal.

I like this girl, not because she's a thousand in one,
But because she's one in a thousand, my chosen one.
And though she may not be a perfect fit,
She's perfect for me, that's for sure, no need to admit.

11. Flicker of Hope

The boy with a heavy heart,
Lost in a sea of pain and hurt.
His love, once so bright and strong,
Now drifted away, leaving him alone.

He sits alone in the darkness,
Wondering where he went wrong.
His dreams shattered, his hopes gone,
He feels like he can't go on.

But something deep inside him stirs,
A flicker of hope, a tiny flame.
He realizes that he's not alone,
And that he can still find his way.

He picks himself up and wipes away his tears,
Determined to face another day.
For he knows that even though love may fade,
Life still holds beauty in its own way.

So he takes a deep breath and looks ahead,
With a newfound strength and resolve.
And even though his heart still aches,
He knows he can overcome.

12. Expired Poison

Once sweet and desirable,
Now bitter to the taste,
A poison, once desired,
Is now a bitter waste.

Like the venom in a serpent's fang,
Or the toxins in a spider's web,
The pain of lost love lingers on,
And fills the heart with dread.

The boy, now broken and alone,
Feels the poison in his veins,
It courses through his body,
And drives him half insane.

He longs to be free of the pain,
To break the shackles of his heart,
But the poison holds him captive,
And tears his soul apart.

He knows that he must move on,
That love will come again,
But for now he's trapped in misery,
A victim of love's cruel game.

So like an expired poison,
He lies in wait, alone,
Hoping that time will heal his wounds,
And help him find his way back home.

13. The Strength to Let Go

The hardest choices require the strongest wills,
To make a decision that your heart fills
With doubt and fear, and pain and strife,
To leave behind a love that's been your life.

It's not easy to move on from a girl you love the most,
To accept that the bond you shared is now a ghost.
It's like walking away from a part of your soul,
Leaving you feeling incomplete and not whole.

But sometimes, to move forward, we must let go,
And find the strength to stand on our own.
For love should never be a source of pain,
It should uplift us and make us feel sane.

So take a deep breath and find your will,
To make the choice that your heart fills
With hope and the promise of a new day,
Where love will come and brighten your way.

14. Echoes of Regret

He walks alone, with heavy steps
His heart still aches, his soul still weeps
He knows he's wrong, but can't confess
The pain he caused, the love he repressed

He didn't treat her well, he knows
He pushed her away, he dealt the blows
But in his heart, he wanted her near
He tried to hold on, but gave in to fear

The breakup left him lost and confused
His actions, rash and often abused
He said things he didn't mean to say
He hurt her deeply, day by day

He thought he could move on, be free
But the reality, he couldn't see
He longs for her touch, her smile, her love
But she's gone, with wings like a dove

Now he sits, alone in his room
Regretting his actions, his own doom
He wishes he could turn back time
To treat her well, and make her mine

But it's too late, the damage is done
The chance is gone, the battle is won
He must learn to live with his regret
And hope that someday, he'll forget.

15. Elegance in Every Fold

I watch her as she walks by,
In her saree, she catches my eye.
Her beauty takes my breath away,
I can't help but admire her today.

Her saree hugs her curves just right,
Her elegance shines in the light.
Every move she makes, so graceful and free,
My heart skips a beat, she's all I see.

I can't help but feel so lucky,
To have her by my side, so lovely.
Her beauty is unmatched, her smile so bright,
In her saree, she's a true delight.

I thank the stars above,
For giving me this girl I love.
In her saree, she's perfect to me,
Forever my heart she'll always be.

16. Whispers of a Hidden Heart

I see her smile, I see her grace,
And I feel my heart begin to race.
But every time I try to speak,
My courage fails, my knees go weak.

I long to tell her how I feel,
But my fear makes me hesitate and kneel,
What if she doesn't feel the same,
What if I'm the only one to blame?

My mind is filled with doubts and fears,
And I struggle to hold back the tears,
For I know that she's the one,
The girl who's captured my heart and won.

I see her every day and night,
And I wonder if she's in my sight,
But I keep my feelings locked away,
And hope that she'll come to me someday.

Until then, I'll keep on dreaming,
Of the day when I'll start believing,
Believing in myself, believing in love,
And finally telling her, my heart's dove.

For she deserves to know the truth,
The feelings that have been hidden since my youth,
And though my fear may be hard to beat,
I'll take the chance, and hope for a sweet retreat.

I'll find the courage to speak my heart,
And pray that we'll never be apart,
For she's the one who's captured my soul,
And I'll tell her soon, to make my heart whole.

17. Seen-Zoned by Destiny: The Desi Heart's Rollercoaster

Oh, yaar, let me tell you, it's such a desi mystery,
Why we fall for the one who's not our destiny!
Of all the fish in the sea, why this one we choose,
The one who gives us "seen" and leaves us confused!

We swipe left, we swipe right, on every app we try,
But our heart goes "Dhak Dhak" for the one who says "Bye!"
They don't text back, they leave us on "blue tick,"
Still, we daydream of them, like some Bollywood flick!

Mummy says, "Beta, find someone nice and steady,"
But no, we want the one who's already ready...
To break our heart, to ghost us, to make us cry,
Yet we chase them like it's a butter chicken fry!

We analyze their stories, their every single post,

"Why did they like that pic? Are we still the most?"
We consult astrologers, pandits, and baba jis,
But destiny laughs and says, "Chill, it's just a phase, ji!"

We know they're not the one, but still, we hope,
Like a roadside chai without any scope.
We ignore the red flags, we ignore the signs,
Because love makes us blind, and also out of our minds!

So here's to the one who's not meant to be,
The one who makes us go "Oh God, why me?"
We'll keep falling, we'll keep trying, till we finally see,
That destiny has someone better, just wait and see!

Till then, let's laugh, let's cry, let's enjoy the ride,
Because love in desi style is always full of pride!
And remember, yaaron, when it's all said and done,
The right one will come, with a "Hi" and not "Hmm..." 😊

18. One-Sided Kick

Oh, the beauty of one-sided love, so pure, so true,
Where I dream of "us," and you dream of... who?
I send you good morning texts, you reply with "Hmm,"
But my heart still skips a beat, like a drunk drummer's
drum!

Your DP changes, and I overanalyze,
"Is that a hint? A secret message for my eyes?"
I stalk your Insta, your tweets, your every move,
While you're out there living life, completely in the
groove.

You post a story, I watch it ten times,
Looking for hidden meanings, decoding your rhymes.
You share a song, and I think, "Is it for me?"
Meanwhile, you're just vibing to the melody!

I gift you chocolates, you say, "Thanks, bro,"
And I die a little inside, but still, I glow.
You talk about your crush, and I play the friend,

Nodding and smiling, while my heart starts to bend.

Mummy says, "Beta, move on, find someone new,"
But how can I, when my heart beats only for you?
You're like that golgappa stall at the end of the lane,
Always out of reach, yet I crave you again!

I write you poems, you read them with a smirk,
And I pretend I'm fine, though I'm going berserk.
You call me "buddy," I call you "my world,"
This one-sided love is a chaos unfurled!

But hey, let's not forget the perks, my friend,
One-sided love is a trend that never ends!
No fights, no drama, no compromises to make,
Just me, my dreams, and the heartbreaks I fake.

So here's to the beauty of unrequited love,
A gift from the heavens, or maybe above.
It's messy, it's crazy, it's a rollercoaster ride,
But in this desi love story, I'll always take pride!

Because one day, maybe, just maybe, you'll see,
The one who's been loving you blindly is me.
Till then, I'll keep smiling, I'll keep hoping, I'll stay,
Living in my one-sided love, the desi way! 😊